The Days of the DINOSAUR
Coloring Book

by Matthew Kalmenoff

DOVER PUBLICATIONS, INC., New York

CLASSIFICATION OF THE DINOSAURS AND RELATED ANIMALS

(the numbers always refer to the *left-hand* page of the appropriate double-page drawing or the specific page of the single-page drawings)

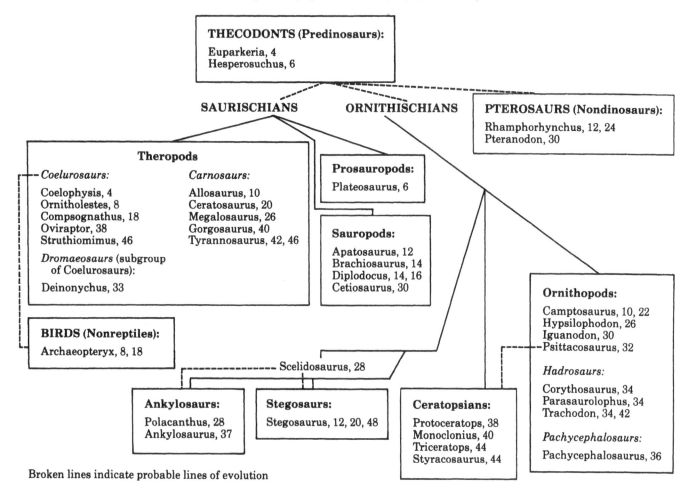

THECODONTS (Predinosaurs):
Euparkeria, 4
Hesperosuchus, 6

SAURISCHIANS

ORNITHISCHIANS

PTEROSAURS (Nondinosaurs):
Rhamphorhynchus, 12, 24
Pteranodon, 30

Theropods

Coelurosaurs:
Coelophysis, 4
Ornitholestes, 8
Compsognathus, 18
Oviraptor, 38
Struthiomimus, 46

Dromaeosaurs (subgroup of Coelurosaurs):
Deinonychus, 33

Carnosaurs:
Allosaurus, 10
Ceratosaurus, 20
Megalosaurus, 26
Gorgosaurus, 40
Tyrannosaurus, 42, 46

Prosauropods:
Plateosaurus, 6

Sauropods:
Apatosaurus, 12
Brachiosaurus, 14
Diplodocus, 14, 16
Cetiosaurus, 30

Ornithopods:
Camptosaurus, 10, 22
Hypsilophodon, 26
Iguanodon, 30
Psittacosaurus, 32

Hadrosaurs:
Corythosaurus, 34
Parasaurolophus, 34
Trachodon, 34, 42

Pachycephalosaurs:
Pachycephalosaurus, 36

BIRDS (Nonreptiles):
Archaeopteryx, 8, 18

Scelidosaurus, 28

Ankylosaurs:
Polacanthus, 28
Ankylosaurus, 37

Stegosaurs:
Stegosaurus, 12, 20, 48

Ceratopsians:
Protoceratops, 38
Monoclonius, 40
Triceratops, 44
Styracosaurus, 44

Broken lines indicate probable lines of evolution

The Days of the Dinosaur Coloring Book is a new work, first published by Dover Publications, Inc., in 1987.

International Standard Book Number

ISBN-13: 978-0-486-25359-6
ISBN-10: 0-486-25359-7

Manufactured in the United States by LSC Communications
25359720   2018
www.doverpublications.com

Publisher's Note

In or around 1820, Mary Ann Mantel, the wife of an English surgeon and amateur paleontologist, found a large fossilized reptilian tooth in a pile of stones in Sussex, England. It turned out to be the tooth of the first recognized dinosaur, Iguanodon. This discovery marked the beginning of the study of dinosaurs, which before then were not known to have existed. From that moment on, dinosaurs have fascinated mankind. They have captivated our curiosity, scientific and otherwise, and our imagination.

And now, at a time when space flights and technological advances speed us inexorably into the future, we are drawn as never before to these beasts of the past. From the most devoted paleontologist who seeks answers to possibly unanswerable questions to the awestruck child who revels in the knowledge that these huge monsters were real, we endeavor to know all we can about the dinosaurs, and the more we know about them, the more wonder and respect they inspire in us. It is not difficult to see why they affect us so: They lived an almost inconceivably long time ago, they were so unlike all other animals mankind has ever known and they came to an unexplained end after a tremendously long existence. Dinosaurs of one kind or another survived for a period of 160 million years, and for most of that time they dominated all other life forms on the earth, including the then lowly mammals. (By comparison, mankind has inhabited the planet for less than 2 million years.) After their long reign, however, the dinosaurs mysteriously and rather abruptly (as geologic time goes) died off completely, leaving behind only a legacy of long-buried relics for Mrs. Mantel and others to discover. From these relics we have learned much.

The division of geologic time in which the dinosaurs lived is known as the Mesozoic Era (from 248 to 65 million years ago), a time span that encompassed three periods: the Triassic (248 to 213 million years ago), the Jurassic (213 to 144 million years ago) and the Cretaceous (144 to 65 million years ago). The first dinosaurs appeared in the latter half of the Triassic Period. At that time the earth's climate was predominantly warm and wet, and an abundance of large auracarian trees, primitive conifers and cycads, as well as ferns, rushes and horsetails characterized the flora. The Jurassic Period, a time when most types of dinosaurs flourished, was marked by many tropical lowlands and swamps. Ferns, conifers, cycads and other gymnosperms were typical plants. The Cretaceous Period for the most part saw the dinosaurs continue to thrive and diversify. It was a time in which the earth's climate cooled and became conducive to many modern flowering plants, such as laurel, and to the familiar magnolia, oak, willow and sassafras trees, as well as conifers, ferns and other low plants. However, by the end of the Cretaceous Period, the dinosaurs had become extinct, and, despite numerous theories, scientists are still unable to fully explain their sudden disappearance. (One of the most widely accepted theories maintains that the earth became inhabitable to the dinosaurs as a result of the impact of a huge asteroid, which would have thrown enough dust into the atmosphere to envelop the earth in darkness for months.)

Dinosaurs were reptiles. The name dinosaur means "terrible lizard" and is actually a collective term referring to two separate groups of reptiles, the saurischians ("lizard hips") and the ornithischians ("bird hips"). As their names suggest, the pelvic bones of the saurischians and ornithischians were arranged differently. The chart on the preceding page shows to which group the dinosaurs covered in this book belong.

Almost all we know about dinosaurs comes from the study of their fossilized remains. That we know as much as we do about these bizarre creatures, the last of which died over 64 million years ago, is a tribute to those paleontologists who have spent untold hours in the field recovering dinosaur fossils and in the laboratory studying them and piecing the specimens together. Using the fossilized bones, scientists are able to reconstruct the skeletons of these animals, from which much can be determined: how large the animal was, whether it had a long tail or neck, the length of its limbs, what means of defense it might have employed, even what it ate. Fossils, however, cannot tell us everything about dinosaurs (see page 48). Ultimately much of the appearance and many of the characteristics assigned by scientists to specific dinosaurs are based largely on educated suppositions, which sometimes conflict with the educated suppositions of other scientists. Occasionally new discoveries prove everyone wrong; at the very least they almost always give rise to further rounds of hypothesizing. Basically still in its infancy, the study of dinosaurs is an ongoing one; there remains much to be learned.

The dinosaurs pictured in this book were carefully researched and precisely rendered by Matthew Kalmenoff, a former staff artist at the American Museum of Natural History in New York City. They are presented in roughly chronological order, illustrating the evolution of the dinosaurs and related animals, from their Triassic thecodont ancestors and the early saurischians that evolved from them, to the many diverse forms of saurischians, ornithischians and flying creatures that flourished in the Jurassic Period, and on through the Cretaceous Period to those relatively advanced genera that lived right up to the time of the dinosaurs' extinction. Covering two pages each (with few exceptions), the illustrations depict 32 dinosaurs, 2 flying reptiles, 2 ancestral reptiles and 1 primitive bird in their natural habitats. Remember as you color the various prehistoric animals that scientists have no means of determining their actual skin colors; let your imagination be your guide. The captions provide interesting information on each of the Mesozoic creatures you'll find here, as you journey back in time millions of years to those days when great reptilian beasts walked the earth, the days of the dinosaur!

Euparkeria *(left),* a reptile that first appeared in the early Triassic Period, was probably an ancestor of the major reptilian groups of the Mesozoic Era, including the dinosaurs. Called a *thecodont* because its teeth were implanted in sockets, Euparkeria (yu-park-ER-ee-yuh, "Parker's true reptile"—named in honor of morphologist W. Kitchen Parker) grew to a length of 3 feet and lived on lizards and large insects, chasing them down on its powerful hind legs. **Coelophysis** *(right),* was one of the first dinosaurs. It lived during the Triassic Period and belonged to a group of dinosaurs called *coelurosaurs.* These dinosaurs were small, agile carnivores that could run very rapidly on their hind legs. Coelophysis (see-loh-FY-sis, "hollow form") was 8 feet long and 3 feet high, but weighed less than 80 pounds, partly because it had hollow bones.

Hesperosuchus *(left),* like Euparkeria, was a Triassic bipedal thecodont that lived alongside many of its descendants, including several genera of dinosaurs. Approximately 5 feet in length, Hesperosuchus (hes-per-oh-SU-kus, "western crocodile") was a quick, agile predator, able to pursue small reptiles and amphibians on its strong hind limbs. It used its smaller forelimbs to grasp and hold its prey when feeding. **Plateosaurus** *(right),* a late Triassic herbivore that measured 23 feet in length, is placed by some authorities in a small group of dinosaurs called *prosauropods,* thought to be ancestors of the much larger sauropods, such as Apatosaurus and Brachiosaurus. Plateosaurus (plat-ee-oh-SAWR-us, "flat lizard") normally walked on all four legs, but could rear up on its hind legs to feed or move quickly.

6

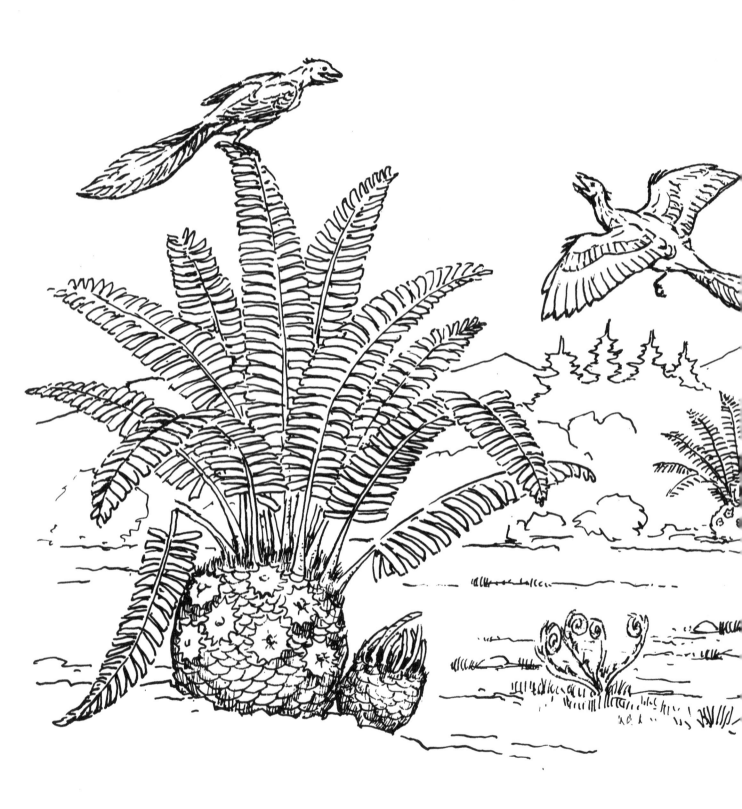

The flesh-eating dinosaurs, known as *theropods*, fall into two groups: the large, formidable carnosaurs, such as Allosaurus and Tyrannosaurus, and the small, nimble coelurosaurs. **Ornitholestes** was one of the largest of the coelurosaurs, ranging in length from 6 to 10 feet. Like its ancestor Coelophysis, it was light in weight and extremely swift, so that it could feed on small reptiles, primitive mammals and early birds, such as **Archaeopteryx** (see also page 18). Ornitholestes (or-nith-oh-LES-teez, "bird robber") lived during the Jurassic Period.

Allosaurus was one of the fiercest and most dominant Jurassic members of the group of theropods known as *carnosaurs*, the giant hunters of the Mesozoic Era. Allosaurus (al-loh-SAWR-us, "different lizard") was a formidable animal, up to 40 feet in length, 30 feet in height and 5 tons in weight, and yet, despite its size, it could attain speeds comparable to those of a swift person. Its huge razor-sharp teeth, massive jaws and enormous claws on its forelimbs enabled it to rip large chunks of flesh from its victims, which included the great vegetarian dinosaurs of the period, such as Apatosaurus and Diplodocus. The victim shown here, over which a confrontation appears imminent, is **Camptosaurus** (see page 22).

Apatosaurus *(left),* also commonly called **Brontosaurus** (brahn-toh-SAWR-us, "thunder lizard"), is probably the best-known dinosaur. Like the other sauropods, those gigantic familiarly shaped quadrupedal creatures with their long necks and tails, huge bodies and disproportionately small heads, Apatosaurus (uh-pat-oh-SAWR-us, "deceptive lizard") was a herbivore that, while capable of walking on land, probably also sought food and refuge in water. It attained a length of 70 feet and weighed up to 30 tons. Fossilized footprints indicate that most Jurassic sauropods probably traveled in herds. Also pictured are **Stegosaurus** *(right;* see page 20) and (in the sky) **Rhamphorhynchus** (see page 24).

Brachiosaurus *(left)* was the most massive of the known sauropods and possibly the largest animal that ever lived. It weighed up to 85 tons and, despite its relatively short tail, measured up to 100 feet in length. Strictly herbivorous, Brachiosaurus (brak-ee-oh-SAWR-us, "arm lizard") lived during the Jurassic Period and probably split its time equally between the land and the water. High shoulders, long forelimbs and nostrils located high up on its skull distinguished it from other sauropods—**Diplodocus** *(right;* see page 16), for example.

Diplodocus, although almost as long as the huge Brachiosaurus, was one of the least massive of all the Jurassic-era sauropods, weighing no more than 20 tons. Of its 90-foot length, the tail and neck accounted for over 70 feet. (The tail was 45 feet and the neck 26 feet.) Similar in habit to the other sauropods, Diplodocus (dip-loh-DAHK-us, "double-beam") probably spent nearly equal portions of each day foraging for vegetation on land and resting in bodies of shallow water. Unlike other sauropods, its teeth were positioned solely at the front of its jaws.

Archaeopteryx, one of the earliest and most primitive birds known, lived during the Jurassic Period. Featuring both reptilian and avian characteristics, it is regarded by many paleontologists as the evolutionary link between reptiles and birds. Its weak wing structure indicates that Archaeopteryx (ar-kee-AHP-ter-iks, "ancient wing") was incapable of sustained

flight. **Compsognathus**, the smallest known dinosaur, was approximately the size of a large chicken. Like its relative Ornitholestes, this Jurassic coelurosaur was able to move quickly on its hind legs either in pursuit of its prey or in flight from its enemies. Compsognathus (kahmp-SAHG-nuh-thus, "pretty jaw") probably fed on insects, small lizards and mammals.

Stegosaurus *(left),* another well-known dinosaur, was the largest known member of the group of herbivorous armored dinosaurs called *stegosaurs*. It was about 20 feet long, weighed slightly less than 2 tons and featured a double row of diamond-shaped bony plates along its back and two pairs of large spikes near the end of its tail. The spikes were obviously lethal weapons against predators but the bony plates are less easily explained (see page 48). They were possibly a form of protective armor or, more likely, a means of controlling body temperature. Although Stegosaurus (STEG-oh-sawr-us, "cover lizard") roamed North America, Eurasia and Africa in large numbers during the Jurassic Period, by early Cretaceous times it was extinct.
Ceratosaurus *(right)* was a large, savage carnivore, similar in size and habits to the other formidable carnosaurs of the Jurassic Period, such as Allosaurus. The bladelike horn on its nose and the bony knobs above its eyes distinguished Ceratosaurus (seh-rat-oh-SAWR-us, "horned lizard") from its relatives.

Camptosaurus lived during the Jurassic Period and belonged to the group of dinosaurs called *ornithopods,* the most abundant dinosaurian suborder of Jurassic and Cretaceous times. Ornithopods probably moved about on four legs but reared up on two when necessary to feed or to run. They had horny beaks, used for eating plants, and their forelimbs, while not as large as their hind legs, were very useful for pulling and holding foliage. Camptosaurus (KAMP-toh-sawr-us, "bent lizard"), a rather primitive ornithopod, ranged in length from 10 to 16 feet and weighed about half a ton.

Rhamphorhynchus was an early type of flying reptile or *pterosaur* that lived during the middle Jurassic Period. Like other pterosaurs, it was lightly built and hollow-boned and had extremely thin wings that were supported by the greatly elongated fourth-finger bones of its hands. Rhamphorhynchus (ram-foh-RINK-us, "prow beak") was about 2 feet long, and probably glided as often as it flew by flapping its wings. The flat disc at the end of its long tail probably served as a steering device. The animals in the water are some type of sauropod.

Hypsilophodon *(left)* was a 6½-foot-long primitive ornithopod whose relatively lengthy existence—from the Jurassic through the early Cretaceous—demonstrated that being small in an environment dominated by large predators was not necessarily a disadvantage, especially if the smallness was accompanied, as in Hypsilophodon's case, by swiftness and agility. An otherwise defenseless herbivore, Hypsilophodon (hip-sil-LOH-foh-dahn, "high-crested tooth")

was lightweight and able to outrun or outdodge most of its enemies. **Megalosaurus** *(right)*, the first dinosaur to be named, was another long-lived dinosaur that first appeared in the early Jurassic and lasted through the early Cretaceous. About 30 feet in length and weighing as much as a moderate-sized elephant, Megalosaurus (meg-uh-loh-SAWR-us, "big lizard") was a formidable carnosaur with large, sharp teeth and wide jaws.

Paleontologists divide the armored dinosaurs into two groups known as the *stegosaurs* and the *ankylosaurs*. The culmination of the stegosaur line was Stegosaurus, which apparently died out early in the Cretaceous Period. Its place in the ecological system was probably taken by the ankylosaur line, which, according to the fossil record, appeared at that time. Both groups of dinosaurs possibly evolved from **Scelidosaurus** *(right),* a primitive armored dinosaur that first appeared in the early Jurassic Period and that demonstrated characteristics common to the two later groups of armored dinosaurs. Scelidosaurus (skeh-LY-doh-sawr-us, "limb reptile") was

covered from head to tail with bony plates, including a vertically situated row of bony plates along the top and bottom of its tail. About 13 feet in length, it lumbered along on all fours and ate soft vegetation. **Polacanthus** *(left)* was an early Cretaceous ankylosaur. Its protective armor was noticeably more developed than that of Scelidosaurus and Stegosaurus. Its body was covered with bony armor plates, and along its back ran two rows of large spikes with two additional rows of vertical plates lining the top of the tail. Polacanthus (pohl-uh-KAN-thus, "many spikes") measured 15 feet in length, traveled on all fours and fed on plants.

Iguanodon *(left)* was an early Cretaceous ornithopod, about 30 feet in length, 5 tons in weight and 15 feet in height. It featured spiked thumbs that were probably used as defensive weapons. Iguanodon (ih-GWAHN-oh-dahn, "iguana tooth") is an especially significant dinosaur because it was the discovery of its fossilized teeth in or around 1820 that marked the beginning of the study of dinosaurs, which were not known to have existed before that time. **Pteranodon** (in the sky), perhaps the best-known pterosaur, was a Cretaceous descendant of Rhamphorhynchus. It had a wingspan of 25 feet and weighed 40 pounds. Pteranodon (teh-RAN-oh-dahn, "winged-toothless") used its thin-skinned wings primarily to glide, and probably relied on the long bony crest on top of its skull to balance its long toothless jaws when diving for fish. **Cetiosaurus** *(right)*, a typical sauropod, reached lengths of 50 feet. The giant sauropods, after attaining their peak in the Jurassic Period, declined greatly in number during the Cretaceous Period; however, a few genera may have persisted up to the dinosaurs' mass extinction. Cetiosaurus (seh-tee-oh-SAWR-us, "whale reptile") was the first sauropod named, at a time when sauropods were thought to be entirely aquatic animals.

Psittacosaurus, a late Cretaceous herbivore, is considered by many authorities to be a possible evolutionary link between the ornithopods and the group of large herbivorous horned dinosaurs that would evolve later, called *ceratopsians*. About 5 or 6 feet in length, Psittacosaurus (sit-uh-koh-SAWR-us, "parrot lizard"), like other ornithopods, was partly bipedal; yet it also had many features that foreshadowed the development of the ceratopsians: a parrotlike beak, relatively elongated and strong forelimbs and a high, narrow skull with a bony ridge across the back of it.

Deinonychus was an early Cretaceous member of a branch of the coelurosaurs called *dromaeosaurs,* a group of dinosaurs that were highly specialized predators. For example, Deinonychus (dy-noh-NYK-us, "terrible claw"), an extremely swift and ferocious bipedal carnivore, wielded a unique weapon adapted for one purpose: having latched on to its prey with its forelimb claws, Deinonychus employed the sickle-shaped inner claw on each of its hind feet to rip open its victim. Deinonychus measured approximately 9 feet in length, stood about 5 feet high and weighed less than 200 pounds.

Corythosaurus *(left)*, **Parasaurolophus** *(second from right)* and **Trachodon** *(far right)*, also called **Anatosaurus** (uh-nat-oh-SAWR-us, "duck lizard"), all belonged to a group of ornithopod dinosaurs called *hadrosaurs*. These were late Cretaceous herbivores characterized by pebbly skin, ducklike bills and distinctive bony head crests. The exact purpose of the elaborate head crests, some of which were hollow, is not known. One theory suggests that the crests contained sensory tissue, providing hadrosaurs with a keen sense of smell. Other theories suggest that the diverse crests developed to enable different genera to recognize their own kind, or that they served as resonators to amplify mating or warning calls. Corythosaurus (kor-ith-oh-SAWR-us, "helmet lizard") was 25 feet long; Parasaurolophus (par-uh-saw-RAHL-oh-fus, "close-to-lizard crest") was 30 feet long; and Trachodon (TRAK-oh-dahn, "rough tooth"), a flat-headed hadrosaur with no elaborate crest, was 40 feet long.

Pachycephalosaurus belonged to a small group of ornithopod dinosaurs called *pachy-cephalosaurs*. These Cretaceous dinosaurs were unique in that the tops of their skulls were extremely thick. It is thought that the male pachycephalosaurs butted heads during mating season, much like modern wild goats and sheep. The skull of Pachycephalosaurus (pak-ee-SEF-uh-loh-sawr-us, "thick-headed lizard"), the largest known pachycephalosaur, was up to 10 inches thick, and its snout and the back of its skull were covered with bony bumps and spikes. Pachycephalosaurus reached lengths of up to 26 feet.

Ankylosaurus was a late Cretaceous relative of the earlier ankylosaur Polacanthus. The top of its broad, massive body was covered by a coat of armor consisting of flexible bony plates, and its sides were protected by a series of large horizontally positioned spikes. When confronted by a predator, Ankylosaurus (AYN-kil-oh-sawr-us, "crooked lizard") probably lowered its 3-ton, 18-foot-long body to the ground to protect its vulnerable underbelly and fended off attempts to overturn it with the huge bony club at the end of its tail.

Oviraptor *(left)* was a late Cretaceous coelurosaur that measured 3 to 6 feet in length. Its long, slender legs were clearly suited for running and its long arms and clawed hands were well-suited for grasping. Related to earlier coelurosaurs, such as Coelophysis and Ornitholestes, Oviraptor (oh-vih-RAP-tor, "egg stealer"), as its name suggests, probably used its toothless jaws to feed on the eggs of other dinosaurs. **Protoceratops** *(right)* was one of the earliest members of a group of dinosaurs called *ceratopsians,* the great horned herbivores that possibly evolved from the ornithopod Psittacosaurus during the late Cretaceous Period. Ceratopsians were characterized by a large skull that extended back over the vulnerable neck region into a bony frill. In addition to providing protection, the frill also served as a point of attachment for the powerful neck and jaw muscles. Protoceratops (proh-toh-SEHR-uh-tops, "first horn-face"), at 5 to 7 feet in length and 400 pounds in weight, was small in comparison to its more famous descendants, such as Triceratops, and it did not develop the horns that marked its later relatives.

Monoclonius *(left)* was one of the many genera of ceratopsians that descended from Protoceratops during the late Cretaceous Period. Like the other great horned dinosaurs, Monoclonius (mahn-oh-KLOH-nee-us, "single stem") was a massive creature that probably roamed in herds, feeding on vegetation with its large, powerful parrotlike beak. The single well-developed horn on its nose and the two smaller bony protrusions over the eye sockets distinguished it from its relatives. **Gorgosaurus** *(right),* a huge, formidable carnosaur of Cretaceous times, was a close relative of Tyrannosaurus. About 35 feet long and 12 feet tall, Gorgosaurus (gorg-oh-SAWR-us, "gorgon lizard") traveled on its hind legs and used its powerful jaws and sharp teeth to kill and feed on its victims.

Tyrannosaurus *(left)* was the largest and fiercest known predator dinosaur that ever lived. The evolutionary culmination of the carnosaur line of theropods, Tyrannosaurus (ty-ran-oh-SAWR-us, "tyrant lizard") reigned supreme during Cretaceous times. It stood 16 feet tall, measured over 50 feet in length and weighed up to 10 tons. Its skull was over 4 feet long, with huge gaping jaws that held 60 serrated teeth, some up to 6 inches long. Tyrannosaurus fed on all but the swiftest and most heavily armored dinosaurs, in particular on such large defenseless herbivores as **Trachodon** *(right;* see page 34).

Triceratops *(left),* an easily recognizable dinosaur with its large three-horned head and huge bony frill, was, at 8½ tons, the heaviest known dinosaur apart from the giant sauropods. Triceratops (try-SEHR-uh-tops, "three-horned face") attained a length of 36 feet and, though normally a peaceful herbivore, probably proved more than a match for any Cretaceous predator when provoked. It was one of the last ceratopsians to evolve. **Styracosaurus** *(right)* was

another of the great horned dinosaurs of Cretaceous times. Like the other ceratopsians, Styracosaurus (sty-rak-oh-SAWR-us, "spiky lizard") was fully quadrupedal, with strong, squat limbs, and probably roamed in herds. Measuring 18 feet in length, it used its beaklike mouth to slice off the leaves and branches on which it fed. The large horn on its nose and the impressive spikes on its frill provided protection from attacks by large carnosaurs.

The theropods were in many respects the most successful of all the dinosaurs. The formidable carnosaurs, here represented by their final known member, **Tyrannosaurus** *(left; see page 42),* dominated each period in which they lived. The relatively small, always swift and agile coelurosaurs were the first dinosaurs to appear and they lived up to the end of dinosaur times. One of the last known coelurosaurs was **Struthiomimus** *(right).* This late Cretaceous dinosaur was similar in size and habits to the modern ostrich. Struthiomimus (stru-thee-oh-MY-mus, "ostrich mimic") fed on small prey, eggs, fruit and insects.

Reconstructed skeletons, like this one of Stegosaurus, are useful tools in the study of dinosaurs. However, they cannot tell us everything: the color of the skin or eyes, whether or not the animal had fleshy body parts unsupported by bone, and the purpose of certain body parts. In the case of Stegosaurus, exactly how the diamond-shaped plates along its back served the animal remains a mystery, and perhaps always will. Some recent theories suggest that Stegosaurus had but a single row of plates, and that the plates served as solar panels for heating and cooling the body.